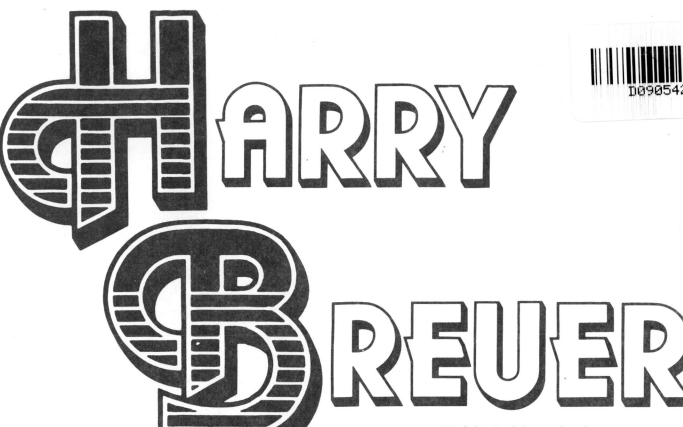

HARRY BREUER'S

MALLET SOLO COLLECTION
For Any Keyboard Percussion Instrument

The collection features Harry Breuer's greatest mallet solos. The solos and piano accompaniments have been totally re-engraved and printed on high quality paper. Solos include: BACK TALK, BIT O' RHYTHM, HAPPY HAMMERS, ON THE WOODPILE, POWDER PUFF, along with two new works—ENCORE-ELISE and THE 1908 RAG.

The xylophone solos in this collection are typical of the playing styles in vogue during the 1920's and 30's. In the early days of broadcasting the xylophone proved to be one of the most popular instruments on the radio. The crisp brillant sound of the wooden bars came through the earphones and primitive speakers with a clarity that other instruments lacked. For program material, most xylophonists preferred up tempo solos with fast variations. In reviewing a radio performance of ''Happy Hammers'' and ''Powder Puff'' a critic wrote: ''It seemed as if the soloist, in some selections, was trying to cram as many notes as possible into each bar.''

Numbers like ''Bit O'Rhythm'' and ''On the Woodpile'' were less flashy, not overloaded with notes, putting emphasis on rhythmic patterns rather than runs and embellishments. In ''Back Talk'' - *jazz licks* (as they were called in the pre-swing era) and dixieland figures are combined to create a musical dialogue.

Rags were always a favorite source of material for xylophone solos. ''The 1908 Rag'' (a xylophonistic version of ''Wild Cherries'') was perhaps one of the most performed rags during the heyday of the ragtime era. From a later period of time (1940's) ''Encore-Elise'' is a rhythmic parody of Van Beethoven's Fur Elise. Although for marimba or vibe, it is playable on xylophone but sounding one octave higher.

Harry Breuer

Harry Breuer was born in Brooklyn, New York on October 24, 1901. He began his musical endeavors with the violin, but at age 13, the xylophone caught his interest, and he made his musical debut as soloist at the New York Academy of Music in 1919. The 20's found him as a pioneer radio broadcaster and soloist in such movie palaces as Radio City Music Hall and others in the East and Midwest. His career in music is multi-faceted: composer of mallet solos, appearances in film shorts and educational films, soloist on recordings, staff percussionist at NBC, and recently, composer and performer of electronic music for European radio, television, and film. Harry who was recently elected into the Percussive Arts Society Hall of Fame, resides on Long Island, New York.

CONTENTS

BACK TALK

Piano Acc.

HARRY BREUER

4

Back Talk-3

BIT O' RHYTHM

Piano Acc.

HARRY BREUER

Bit O' Rhythm-2

8

Bit O' Rhythm-3

Bit O' Rhythm-4

ENCORE-ELISE

Piano Acc.

with apologies
to Van Beethoven
Arr. HARRY BREUER

12

Encore-Elise-4

HAPPY HAMMERS

Piano Acc.

HARRY BREUER

Happy Hammers-2

Trio

(Piano)

57 (Solo)

57

Happy Hammers-4

18

THE 1908 RAG
(Wild Cherries)

Piano Acc.

Moderato

HARRY BREUER

Xylophone
Solo

Piano Acc.

The 1908 Rag-2

The 1908 Rag-3

22

The 1908 Rag-4

ON THE WOODPILE

Piano Acc.

HARRY BREUER

24

On the Woodpile-2

Trio

26

On the Woodpile-4

POWDER PUFF

Piano Acc.

HARRY BREUER

28

Powder Puff-2

Powder Puff-3

30

Powder Puff-4

Powder Puff-5

Coda

Coda

D.S. al fine, poi la Coda.

D.S. al fine, poi la Coda.

Powder Puff-6